BOBBY BENDICK'S RIDE

a poem by
PETER BENNET
with drawings by
BIRTLEY ARIS

When thou shalt come into the marriage chamber, thou shalt take the ashes of perfume, and lay upon them some of the heart and liver of the fish, and shalt make a smoke with it. And the devil shall smell it and flee away.

Tobit 6:16-17

First published in Great Britain in 2010 by Enchiridion,
15 Connaught Gardens, Forest Hall, Newcastle upon Tyne NE12 8AT

Typeset by T. F. P. Workshop Ltd
Cover design by Birtley Aris
Printed in Great Britain by Tyneside Free Press

A CIP catalogue record for this book
is available from the British Library.
ISBN 0 9567147 0 1

Copyright © Peter Bennet and Birtley Aris 2010
All rights reserved.
Peter Bennet and Birtley Aris have exerted their moral rights in
accordance with the Copyright, Designs and Patents Act of 1988.

Shoes grip cobbles to a car-horn tucket.
Nine crocodiles, *monsieur le prêtre*,
are ancient monuments of France. Hearts trip
along a rank of drums. The precious luggage,
Christ, His Mother, and a silk-lined turtle shell,
is shouldered, staggering in air
against the weight of which a fan
stirs damp aromas of the *plat du jour
traditionnel*, peculiar
to this vicinity. Marmot perhaps.
Blood pudding possibly. Identity
is not presumed upon. Our rendezvous
shall be the foyer of La Belle Hôtesse.

> *A muckle beast wi' fowre guid legs
> is Bobby Bendick's mare,
> but Auld Nip loups on twa cleft hooves
> an' follows Bobby far.*

Sometimes in reading and in walking I arrive
as of a sudden at a place in part
familiar and yet not clearly known
and hear my footsteps die away
ahead of me. Uncommon heat
is tightening the strings of summer's
theorbo. The swift-winged choirs
are over Otterburn that are not birds
nor are they cherubim. They see us plod
or jig like pismires on the molehill earth
that trammels us. I now perceive
that by remaining fools we may prevail.
A thin voice stretches and is broken.

> *A muckle beast wi' twa guid lugs*
> *is Bobby Bendick's mare,*
> *but Nip whae wears baeth lugs an' horns*
> *heors Bobby from afar.*

What stirs the air? I know this floor
on which my shadow moves. The huntsman's leg
bends through a crutch below the knee.
He is composed of tesserae
no one has seen who knows his name
for seven hundred years. He draws his bow
and eyes the buck. Who is the last
one to forget? The fish. Fine pleasances
are hereabouts I studied in
of sweet grass in the shade bestowed by oaks
and chestnuts. *L'enfant Enric* himself was not
more comfortable in his *carapace*
than I in those days with my head in books.

> *A muckle beast wi' twa guid een*
> *is Bobby Bendick's mare,*
> *but Nip wi' een like spairkin' lamps*
> *spies Bobby from afar.*

I am a gentleman the Lord has made
uncommon apt to read and walk at once
provided only that my pace
be easy and be regular. Vile Azariah
is no man but a crocodile
in his duplicity. My Bible goes
with me most often and has gathered grass
between its leaves, and such a harvest
of hedgerow foliage withal
to mark those passages I have discovered
most like to veins of profitable ore
that it has now a rustick look
in colour earthen, a most precious clod.

> *A muckle tail to thresh the air*
> *has Bobby Bendick's mare,*
> *but Auld Nip's tail's a muckle flail*
> *tae thresh puir Bobby sore.*

What man would not delight, placed in a garden
to make a survey of its rich collections?
Would groves and grottoes and the artful
wilds of it, the patterned flowers
and open vistas not delight his soul?
How tempting it is then to envy
the all-contriving Genius and strive
by stealth to steal away His secret treasure.
But might the man yet find himself
drawn back towards the gate he entered by
to find that now there is no gate
and where he came by is a darker path?
The reader casts a shadow on the page.

> *A foal o' fair Northumberland*
> *is Bobby Bendick's mare,*
> *but Bobby gans awa' tae France*
> *an' skules wi' Ezra theor.*

Gargoyles like crocodiles weep kisses
upon Sophia's upturned face –
where she is letting down her hair and sings
her secret names while clambering
the nine rungs of the shadow of a ladder –
and kisses on the cheeks of cobblestones.
I see her lean unsteadily
towards the dish of strawberries
I set out on my window-sill.
The Lisles Burn is descending in its linns
to fishponds and a dovecote. Now her song
is silenced by the roaring flutter
that dusts me in my stride and passes over.

> *True-hairted an' a Christian steed*
> *is Bobby Bendick's mare,*
> *she'll kick hor stable door tae spelks*
> *if Ezra passes neor.*

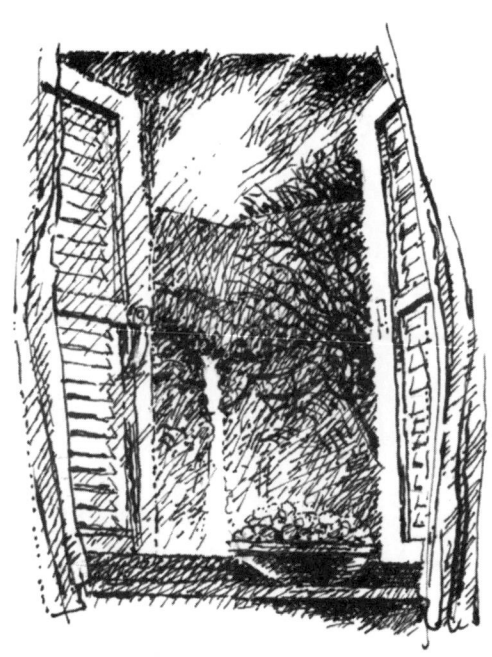

Acquaint me with her words. Her strawberry lips.
A brazier glows. Today the path
where white dust alternates with tender spots
of coolness in which shadows linger
has led to Woodburn or Lescar
and some small industry about an engine
compact of beams and ropes upon a husting
that has a purpose I shall ascertain
by asking. I am a priest and shall be told.
The fish that bit away the foot
shall not be captured but another
filleted for gall and heart and liver
according to the scheme of Azariah.

> *A loyal an' a jealous steed*
> *is Bobby Bendick's mare,*
> *if wicked Ezra tries tae moont*
> *betimes he's kicked awa'.*

I'll hire a car and drive to Paradise
through lynchet-meadows. In a pool
while bathing an offensive-looking trout
will no doubt speak to me. I shall be kind.
Responding pleasantly I will suggest
that we are friends and I breathe water
as he does. *Charmant mais sans merci, c'est moi.*
Nine days I shall abide there to perfect
my holiday. I like the music
the torrent makes, the dewy grass,
the early mass of birds, the clouds
snared on the summits in a net of gold.
Monsieur, I spit upon the *plage*.

> *Beneath a bonny rowan tree*
> *stands Bobby Bendick's mare,*
> *but Ezra's i' the Ingram Pool*
> *whilst Bobby droons him theor.*

Sophia has unclothed herself in smoke
of fish guts and incense. La Belle Hôtesse
is shut down and demolished among ghosts
fading from Pau Hunt photographs, plus-fours
and golf-clubs by the bust of Bernadotte.
The left hand of a Cagot pressed to death
upon a husting *lentement*
pour bien décourager les sorcières
is got by Azariah in exchange
for English money. Great wings will beat me down.
My gown and bands, the cloth I wear
protect me. O Beelzebub
make haste to help me. Make me rich.

> *Ezra's stairk across the back*
> *o' Bobby Bendick's mare.*
> *He'll tak the road tae Blaxter Bog*
> *an' dee nae mischief mair.*

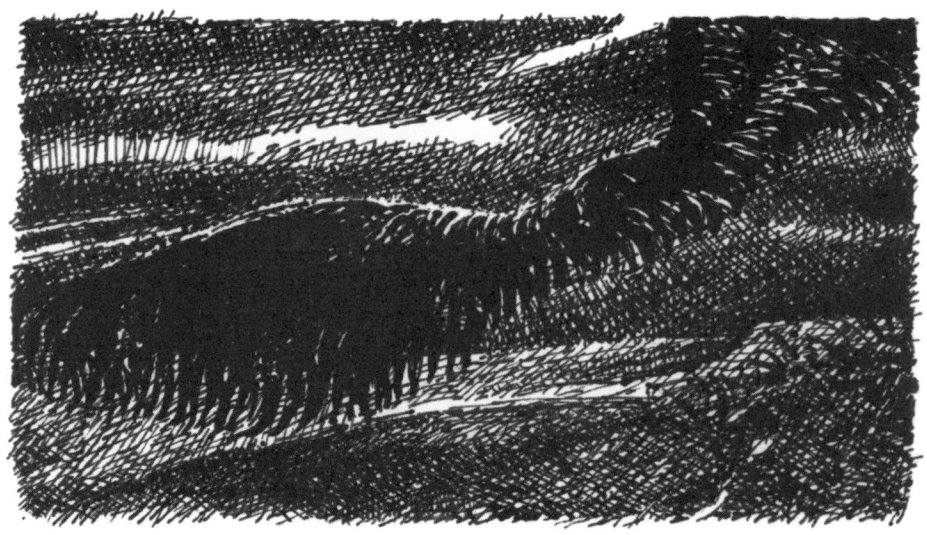

Perceive the world through its disguises.
A ruined church. A ruined priest
to celebrate the Mass for bats. Behold.
This is my parish and my duty.
Look about you, Azariah,
and see a swarm of helicopters drown
in blue air over Corsenside. Today
the wise and merciful Theanthropos
will lead us to the bank of Ingram Pool
and set before us stepping-stones
from which to plunge our crafty souls
again to bathe yet not be cleansed.
I see a blackness and a quivering cloud.

> *By Chairford Bridge an' Grindstone Sike*
> *gans Bobby Bendick's mare,*
> *for Bobby's boond for Wanney Byre*
> *tae hide hissel' awa'.*

Upon a rocking stepping-stone the urge
to stride becomes less marked, yet stride I must.
The golden days go by. The taxi
sinks on its springs. The finest shoe
I ever boned and polished is enshrined
in a broken jar of cassoulet.
What's all this luggage, Azariah,
the nine great crocodiles of France
migrating to the River Rede?
Their hellish jaws. Sometimes a slant of music,
perhaps the Small Pipes, or a known aroma,
or light upon the peaks accuses me.
I am a man whom Wisdom shall reward.

> *By Stiddlehill an' Hepple Heugh*
> *gans Bobby Bendick's mare,*
> *whilst Bobby's grippin' roond hor neck*
> *an' greets wi' mairtal feor.*

The sun each day when it declines
engraves such pictures with a fiery needle
my mind makes on the sweltering clouds
of owl-eyed lust and Azariah
the great fish in a black coat threshing water.
Each night I beat his head again with stones.
He drowned. Yet he returns. The room is empty.
Hark. She sounds. There's nothing there. I am content.
When Wisdom shall again climb through my window
she will converse with me alone.
Monsieur, there's time to take myself to France
and dig a deeper grave. The hand
that rests beside mine on the altar points.

> *A beast wi' teeth like kirkyaird stanes*
> *is Bobby Bendick's mare,*
> *but Auld Nip's like a crocodile*
> *wi' Bobby in his maw.*

Matins at nightfall. Evensong at dawn.
The roof of Cuddy's kirk is gone. Walls totter.
I'll burrow like a marmot at Wanney Byre
before the quick-nosed fiends, the dogs of hell
shall have my blood for pudding. Snares
there are in my resolve, snares in my doubt.
Horizons burn. Hark. The infernal Nimrod
sniffs me out. If God preserve me, let him roar!
Great wings beat down. Virtue decays. The earth
sings psalms to darkness in that quivering cloud
of endless pain and frantic mirth.
No one meddles here but me. The Cagot's hand
points true. My horse is swift. What stirs the air?

> *Nip i' the cleft ca'd Wanney Byre*
> *spares Bobby Bendick's mare,*
> *but hales puir Bobby deun tae hell*
> *wi' Ezra ivor mair.*

The Reverend Robert Bendick and the ballad 'Bobby Bendick's Ride', together with other members of the curious and unlucky Bendick family, are mentioned in *The Silence Room*, a book of short stories by Sean O'Brien. The ballad is not well-known. I think I heard it twenty or thirty years ago in the Gun Inn in Ridsdale on the evening of Bellingham Show, but I may be mistaken. It appears that Bendick studied in France rather than at Oxford or Cambridge, perhaps to save money or to distance himself from scandal. What is known about his family would suggest the latter. His ordination would have taken place during the time of the Commonwealth, though no record of it has been found, and though his activities at and around the Norman church of St Cuthbert at Corsenside cannot be dated with certainty they clearly took place during the long reign of the 'sordid and scandalous' John Graham, who was the curate there from 1617 to 1682, and, we must assume, with his connivance. Bendick was evidently familiar with Pau and the neighbouring town of Lescar, where the mosaic of the crippled huntsman can be seen in the church of Notre-Dame beside the tombs of some of the kings of Navarre. The Musée des Beaux Arts in Pau houses more paintings on the theme of Tobias and the Angel – alias Azariah – than a visitor might expect, no doubt reflecting the interests of a former custodian. The city is also proud to be the birthplace of Henry IV of France, whose cradle was a turtle shell, and of Jean-Baptiste Bernadotte, the sergeant with beautiful legs, who became King of Sweden. A later member of the English colony in Pau was

Major C. W. Mercer, who wrote as Dornford Yates. The genial voice of his creation Bertram 'Berry' Pleydell echoes here and there in the poem. I am indebted to an article by Helen Grant, published in *The Ghosts and Scholars M. R. James Newsletter*, for the information that nine crocodiles are designated ancient monuments in France. According to J. C. Cooper and other authorities, the crocodile symbolises duplicity and viciousness but is also considered to be a guardian of knowledge. The jaws of the crocodile represent hell. Wanney Byre is a fissure in the face of Great Wanney Crag. 'Cuddy's kirk' has been repaired since the time of Robert Bendick, and is used for occasional services. I have been unable to corroborate a report that children in that secretive corner of Northumberland used to be warned to stay away from Ingram Pool after dark for fear of meeting 'Black Bobby'. There are after all less fanciful reasons to avoid deep water at night.

Much of Birtley Aris's work is based on poetry. In the 1970s and 1980s he designed poetry posters for the Mid Northumberland Arts Group, and produced a large number of drawings relating to Edward Thomas's verse. Collaborations with contemporary poets include *Acknowledged Land,* 1994, *Wild,* 2004, with Linda France, *The Railway Sleeper,* 2003, and *Night Train,* 2009, with Sean O'Brien. He lives in Hexham, Northumberland.

Peter Bennet lived near the Wild Hills o' Wanney for over thirty years. His most recent book, *The Glass Swarm,* is a Poetry Book Society Choice and was short-listed for the T. S. Eliot Prize.